Not All Tw

are Jewish

The Lost Ten Tribes of Israel

Igbo Jews

The Igbo Jews of Nigeria claim descent
variously from the tribes
of Ephraim, Naphtali, Menasseh, Levi, Zebulun
and Gad.

Yoruba Jews - *Oyo Empire*

The deportation of the Ten Lost Tribes is
remembered in the tradition preserved by
the palace bards of Oyo as
the Igboho exile.

Dr. Emmanuel Adetula

DR. EMMANUEL ADETULA

President/CEO

Christ Channel Network/CCN House Community Development Agency, CCN Center for Peace and New World Order, Emmanuel Tula Associates

www.christchannelnetwork

www.emmanueltula.com

ISBN: 0-9798136-7-0
ISBN-13: 978-0-9798136-7-2

Dr. Emmanuel Oluwole Adetula

ABOUT CCN CENTER FOR PEACE

CCN Center for Religious Peace is a division of Christ Channel Network (CCN) Inc. It is a bona fide 501(c)(3) nonprofit organization in the United States founded in 2002 by Rev. Emmanuel Adetula .

If you are the one that God is talking to in helping to support this mission, do so today with your financial contribution of any amount to the ministry of Dr. Emmanuel Adetula and the Center for Religious Peace and New World Order. Mail your donation to PO Box 111589, Los Angeles, CA 90011, USA.

www.emmanueltula.com

www.christchannelnetwork.com

www.crpchannel.com

.

CONTENTS

FORWARD

In the late 1800's some clay Assyrian cuneiform tablets were discovered and they were finally translated in the 1930's. These tablets were Assyrian records of this 700's BCE Israelite deportation. There were records of four deportations, which proved the ten tribes of the northern Nation of Israel were assembled into Assyrian culture and became identifiable as the Camerians, the Sycthians, and the Goths. Records of ancient history show that over several hundred years, and through different paths, the Sycthian, Camerian and the Goths migrated essentially to northwest Europe and became known as the Anglo-Saxon Celtic people.

Linguistic analysis of the word "Anglo-Saxon" shows the word "Saxon" means "sons of Isaac." This is exactly what was promised to Abraham and again to Jacob: **Gen. 48:16** "The Angel which redeemed me from all evil, bless the lads; and let my name be named on them, and the name of my fathers Abraham and Isaac; and let them grow into a multitude in the midst of the earth."

Our Creator's statement to Abraham, "in Isaac shall your seed be called" has now happened exactly that way. The basic message the CREATOR was relaying through Abraham is, "That through Isaac the Children of Israel will be able to learn their identity."

Secular history traces the Anglo-Saxon "lost ten tribes" of Israel through the Caucasus Mountains, where they picked up the name Caucasians. From there they migrated into Europe and England. Portions of them migrated from Europe to America. Generally speaking, the democracies of Europe, America, and the countries of the former British Commonwealth are the "lost tribes" of Israel.

In the tradition preserved by the palace bards of Oyo as the Igboho exile, Most African people today originated from the ten lost tribes of Israel and therefore have a share in the blessing of Abraham Most people in these countries have the mistaken feeling that they are gentile because most people today have no idea past two or three generations where they came from. The people of NW Europe migrated to the British Isles, Ireland, and Scotland. They colonized South Africa, New Zealand, Australia, and America. Since they were from the Anglo-Saxon, Celtic people and are called Saxons (sons of Isaac), this is a fulfillment of prophecy. Some of the established Jewish communities existed in such still renowned places as Timbuktu Bamako, and Kano. The UNESCO still maintains notable archives containing records of the old Jewish community of Mali and the Hausa states of Nigeria. For a long time many people have felt there was more to the Hebrew Scriptures (OT) than they have been taught. This is true because the Hebrew Scriptures is written to the people of Israel. Educate yourself on the location of Israel[7] and the truth of *The Holy Scriptures.*

Dr. Emmanuel Oluwole Adetula

In clear contradiction of the Holy Bible; Church leaders and Preachers today pretend that all twelve tribes of Israel are Jewish. Such woefully ignorant or deceptive people deny the biblical distinctions between the 12 Tribes and pretend there's only one tribe: Judah.

Jacob-Israel had 12 sons. Each son became a patriarch of the tribe named after them. For example there's Judah, whose descendants are Jews. There's also Joseph, whose descendants are Joes. Joseph isn't Jewish! , Some Igbos in Nigeria are descendants of Ephraim one of the two sons of Joseph, Ephraim mother was an Egyptian a black woman, Mind you Abraham did have other Baby Mama beside Sarah, just like Moses too was married to a black woman, and later in this book you will see that till today hundreds of spoken words remain the same both in meaning and pronunciation among the Egyptians in Egypt and the people of Owo in Yoruba land of Nigeria.

The 12 Tribes of Israel became the nation of Israel that later split in two: Joseph was the leader of the Northern Kingdom with its 10 tribes, capital Samaria, and Judah was the leader of the Southern Kingdom, capital Jerusalem. The Northern Kingdom of Israel was defeated and deported by the Assyrians 130 years before the Southern Kingdom of Judah was defeated and deported by the Babylonians!

Two separate kingdoms with separate tribes. The Northern Kingdom of Israel became known as the Tribes." The Jews continued to be known as Jews (including exceptions among them to the general rule of relatively few Israelites who sojourned with them).

Not All Twelve Tribes of Israel are Jewish

The first time in the Bible the words "Jews" is used is when the Northern Kingdom of Israel was allied with Syria against the Jews! This is important to note since some deny these great distinctions. The Joes are not and never were Jews! They're Joes.

2 Kings 16:5-6 Then Rezin king of Syria and Pekah son of Remaliah king of Israel came up to Jerusalem to war: and they besieged Ahaz [king of Judah], but could not overcome him. At that time Rezin king of Syria recovered Elath to Syria, and drave the Jews from Elath: and the Syrians came to Elath, and dwelt there unto this day.

Further proof that there are TWELVE TRIBES and not just the Jews/Judah can be found in the distinct blessings of all 12 Tribes by Jacob (Genesis 48-49) and later by Moses (Deuteronomy 32). They're addressed to each of the 12 Tribes of Israel and not just to Judah!

The High Priest had 12 precious gemstones representing the 12 Tribes of Israel - not just one stone in his breastplate, and shouldered two stones with six tribal names on one stone and six tribal names on the other (Exodus 28).

The Promised Land of Israel was divided among the 12 Tribes of Israel, as any biblical map will clearly reveal - not just one big inheritance for Judah.

Ezekiel 47-48 reveals a future division of the Land of Israel again between all 12 Tribes. The New Jerusalem makes mention of 12 Tribes - not just Judah (Revelation 21:12)

Dr. Emmanuel Oluwole Adetula

Those who dare deny these God-given distinctions mentioned in the Bible from Genesis to Revelation pretend all 12 Tribes of Israel have been merged into the one tribe of Judah, denying the distinct biblical prophecies for each of the separate tribes.

Some Jews have a haughty attitude against the other tribes, even against some Jews, and reject the "prodigal son" and would disinherit them contrary to God's Word and Will:

Ezekiel 11:15 "Son of man, your brethren, your relatives, your countrymen, and all the house of Israel in its entirety, are those about whom the inhabitants of Jerusalem have said, 'Get far away from the LORD; this land has been given to us as a possession.'

They want the Gentilized Israelites to remain lost and far away, feeling smug and exclusive, rather than acknowledge they are only a small part of the Chosen People, the Servant Nation, and should seek reconciliation, our family reunion, not further alienation.

Those who pretend that all 12 Tribes are now with Judah speak against the Law and the Prophets that reveal otherwise, as the Law states the People (Am Israel, the Nation or People of Israel - all 12 Tribes) will be restored under King Messiah, and the Prophets speak of two branches representing the two leading tribes of Joseph and Judah being reconciled and reunited.

Conclusive proof Joseph and Judah are still separate and unique identities and tribes:

Ezekiel 37:15-22 The word of the LORD came again unto me, saying, Moreover, thou son of man, take thee one stick, and write upon it, For Judah, and for the children of Israel his companions: then take another stick, and write upon it, For Joseph, the stick of Ephraim and for all the house of Israel his companions: And join them one to another into one stick; and they shall become one in thine hand [they're two sticks, separate but brought together and joined by God].

And when the children of thy people shall speak unto thee, saying, Wilt thou not shew us what thou meanest by these? Say unto them, Thus saith the Lord GOD; Behold, I will take the stick of Joseph, which is in the hand of Ephraim, and the tribes of Israel his fellows, and will put them with him, even with the stick of Judah, and make them one stick, and they shall be one in mine hand.

And the sticks whereon thou writest shall be in thine hand before their eyes. Verse 21 says. And say unto them, Thus saith the Lord GOD; Behold, I will take the children of Israel from among the heathen, whither they be gone, and will gather them on every side, and bring them into their own land: Verse 22 And I will make them one nation in the land upon the mountains of Israel; and one king shall be king to them all: and they shall be no more two nations, neither shall they be divided into two kingdoms any more at all [which division still remains to this day until the restoration of all things].

Some Jews deny Joes are Israelites, and some Joes deny Judah is legitimate, accusing them of being Khazar converts and unworthy of the Jewish Homeland. I refute both hateful teachings with the plain truth of the Bible.

Dr. Emmanuel Oluwole Adetula

In Judaism, there's a concept, "Ma'ase Avot, Siman L'Banim,"the deeds of the fathers are guides for the children. The actions of the forefathers are reflected in the lives of their descendants.

Joseph and Judah fought before and don't always agree today. Joseph's brethren were blind to his identity and Joseph was a world ruler who fed the nations. Some still don't recognize Joseph as the Anglo-Saxons or perceive that Joseph represented Yeshua the Pierced One, but in God's good time all will be revealed beyond any shadow of a doubt.

THE HOUSE OF ISRAEL, which we are considering, is not the same as the House of Judah, of which the Jews were a small remnant only.

The distinction I wish to emphasize is that, while some Jews are Israelites, all Israelites are not necessarily Jews. The House of Judah and some of the Jews are of Israel that is descended, from Jacob. When the general blessings were at Jacob's death apportioned, the 'One Seed' Christ, the Messiah, was promised with the sovereignty to Judah; but the "multitude of nations," most of the spiritual gifts and all the temporal grandeur of the "birthright" were given to the House of Joseph or Ephraim exclusively. The House of Israel was to obtain these in the "latter days" or the Christian era - our days and when developed into a "company of Nations," cf. Imperial Conference of 1926.

The division of Israel took place under the rule of Rehoboam over Judah, Jeroboam over Israel, in 975 B.C. The House of Israel sinned through idolatry and were cast out of the land in 721 B.C. and did not return. The House of Judah also sinned and were punished and banished to Babylon for seventy years, and a remnant of them under Ezra and Nehemiah returned as "the Jews" in 536 B.C. The term "Jews" is never in the Bible applied to the Twelve Tribes or to the Ten-tribe House of Israel. These were to be divorced from the Mosaic law and lost to human history and knowledge, but known to God, re-covenanted in Christ, and to enjoy the Hebrew birthright in the isles of the seas, to be His national evangelists to the world, and the inheritors of the Kingdom of God taken away from the Jews and given to a Nation. It will be shown that the British enjoy all the unconditional promises given to the seed of Abraham in the Christian era and that therefore no other Nation can now replace them as Israel.

It was in 741 B.C. that Isaiah prophesied that "within three score and five years shall Ephraim be broken in pieces, that it be not a people." The final siege of Samaria and the deportation of Israel took place in 721 B.C. Subsequently in 676 B.C. Esar-Haddon completed the work begun and from this date the history of the house of Israel ceases in the Scriptures, and the tale is taken up by Prophecy. Judah was carried captive to Babylon by Nebuchadnezzar in 603 B.C. and the Temple finally destroyed in 586 B.C. The word "Jew" is found for the first time in the Bible in II Kings 16:6, but the Second

Book of Kings was not written till the return of Judah and Benjamin after the end of the Babylonian captivity. God first made his covenant with Abram in Genesis chapters 12-18. In Genesis 17:4-7, God promised Abraham: "As for me, this is my covenant with you: You will be the father of many nations. No longer will you be called Abram; your name will be Abraham, for I have made you a father of many nations. I will make you very fruitful; I will make nations of you, and kings will come from you. I will establish my covenant as an everlasting covenant between

Dr. Emmanuel Oluwole Adetula

me and you and your descendants after you for the generations to come, to be your God and the God of your descendants after you. The whole land of Canaan, where you are now an alien, I will give as an everlasting possession to you and your descendants after you; and I will be their God." (Bold added for emphasis)

CONTRAST BETWEEN ISRAEL AND JEWS

ISRAEL were to be called by a new name (Isa. 62:2). **The Jews** have retained their old name unchanged.

ISRAEL were to be blind to their identity (Rom. 11:25). **The Jews** still claim to be the chosen people.

ISRAEL were to become known as the righteous Nation that keepeth the truth (Isa. 26:2). **The Jews** were to be a reproach and a proverb, a taunt and a curse (Jer. 24:9).

ISRAEL were to become a Nation and a Company of Nations (Gen. 35:11). The Jews were to be scattered in all the "kingdoms of the earth for their hurt" (Jer. 24:9).

ISRAEL were to make a new home in the Appointed Place - the Isles of the Sea (II Sam. 7:10; Isa. 24:15; Isa. 49:1; Jer. 31: 10, etc.).

ISRAEL were to be a Nation for ever (Jer. 31:36). The Jewish nation was broken beyond repair in A.D. 70 (Dan. 9:24; Jer. 1 9: 11).

ISRAEL were to have a perpetual monarchy (Jer. 33:17). The Jews have no king on earth.

ISRAEL were to come under a new covenant (Jer. 31:33). The Jews have remained under the old law.

ISRAEL were to be called the sons of God, i.e. accept Christianity (Hos. 1:10). The Jews do not accept Jesus Christ as the Messiah.

The Northern Kingdom were not, and are not, "Jews"!

The term "Jew" originated from "Judah," one of the tribes of Israel, who, after the twelve tribes of Israel divided into two independent kingdoms, along with the tribe of Benjamin formed the totally-separate-from-Israel "Kingdom of Judah," as this verse which records war between Judah and Israel makes plain:

"When Rehoboam came to Jerusalem, he assembled all the house of Judah [i.e. Jews], and the tribe of Benjamin, a hundred and eighty thousand chosen warriors, to fight against the house of Israel, to restore the kingdom to Rehoboam the son of Solomon." (1 Kings 12:21 RSV)

All Jews Are Israelites, But Not All Israelites Are Jews!

God changed Jacob's name to Israel (Genesis 32:28). Each of Israel's twelve sons (Reuben, Simeon, Levi, Judah, Dan, Naphtali, Gad, Asher, Issachar, Zebulun, Joseph and Benjamin) were founders of one of the tribes of Israel, the Israelites e.g. from Reuben came the Reubenites, from Levi came the Levites, from Judah came the "Jews." Although the tribe of Joseph was later divided into two tribes, Ephraim and Manasseh (Genesis 48:1-20), the number of tribes in the division of the land (see Tribal Lands) remained at twelve, because the tribe of Levi, as the priesthood, were distributed among the other tribes, and had no land allotment of their own.

The Israelites were united as a single kingdom through the reigns of David and Solomon, but after Solomon's death they split into two completely separate and independent kingdoms - the southern kingdom of "Judah," consisting of the tribes of Judah and Benjamin (1 Kings 12:21) with their capital at Jerusalem, and the northern kingdom of "Israel," consisting of the other ten tribes, with their capital up in Samaria. Israel and Judah were never united again (see Kings of Israel and Judah). Surprisingly, they even fought wars against each other from time to time (see Jews At War With Israel). A very important fact that many do not realize is that Judah, that is, the Jewish people of today, are only one of the tribes of Israel - while all Jews are Israelites, not all Israelites are Jews.

Because of their forsaking of Him, God permitted the two kingdoms to be destroyed. First, the northern kingdom of Israel was gradually conquered by the Assyrians (see Ancient Empires - Assyria), and by 721 B.C. they had practically all been taken into exile to Assyria (2 Kings 17:1-23). The vast majority of them never returned, and have become known as the "Lost Ten Tribes of Israel" - which is what is referred to in the Encyclopedia Britannica article quoted in the opening paragraph.

Then, about 135 years later, in 586 B.C., the southern kingdom of Judah was conquered by the Babylonians (see Why Babylon?), and the Jews were taken into captivity to Babylon. The original Temple of God in Jerusalem was destroyed at that time (see Temples and Temple Mount Treasures). The people of the southern kingdom of Judah however did return after the Babylonians fell to the Persians (see Ancient Empires - Persia), and their descendants have become the Jewish people of today.

A supplementary point to the topic of this study is that since that return from the Babylonian exile in the time of Ezra and Nehemiah, the religious practices of the Jewish people have, over

9

the centuries, evolved into something quite different than their ancestors practiced in earlier times - although Moses would definitely recognize such correct doctrines as obedience to the Ten Commandments and observance of the annual Biblical Holy Days, Moses himself would not understand many of the Jewish religious practices of today. Many man-made traditions and customs were gradually added by authorities such as the Pharisees and Sadducees. By the time of Jesus Christ, when the Jewish authorities accused The Lord of breaking the law, much of which was merely their law, not God's, He rebuked His own people for worshiping God according to their own traditions (e.g. Mark 7:6-9).

One of the most fundamental keys to understanding Bible Prophecy is recognizing that although all Jews are Israelites, not all Israelites are Jews. This is an absolutely vital point because many of the end-time prophecies that speak of "Israel" are frequently not referring to the people of Judah, i.e. the Jewish people - religiously, and more importantly, nationally.

The Igbo Jews of Nigeria are one of the components of the Igbo ethnic group. They are said to have migrated from Syrian, Portuguese and Libyan Israelites into West Africa. Historical records shows that this migration started around 740 C.E. According to amateur Jewish Historian and Forensic Science investigator Chinedu Nwabunwanne of Aguleri, who resides in Los Angeles and has researched this subject for more than 15 years at the UCLA libraries in Los Angeles, "the migration started when the forces of Caliph Mohammed -the last leader of the Umayyads- and his Qaysi-Arab supports defeated the Yamani-Arab Umayyads of Syria in 744 C.E; sacked the Yamanis and their Jewish supporters from Syria. The Syrian-Jewish

Dr. Emmanuel Oluwole Adetula

migrant's tribes Dan, Naphtali, Gad, and Asher resettled in Nigeria where they became known as Sambatyon Jews. In 1484 and 1667 Judeans and Zebulonians from Portugal and Libya respectively joined Sambatyon Jews of Nigeria. Thus, Nigerian Jews originated from the following six Israelite tribes: Judah, Dan, Naphtali, Gad, Asher and Zebulon."

Igbo oral legends also state that certain Nri families may be descendants of Levitical priests who migrated from North Africa. However, Chinedu Nwabunwanne, a member of Nri clan disputes the above claim.

Certain Nigerian communities with Judaic practices have been receiving help from individual Israelis and American Jews who work in Nigeria, out-reach organizations like Kulanu, and African-American Jewish communities in America. Jews from outside Nigeria founded two synagogues in Nigeria, which are attended and maintained by Igbos. Because no formal census has been taken in the region, the number of Igbos in Nigeria who identify as either Israelites or Jews is not known. There are currently 26 synagogues of various sizes. Some researchers estimate there may be as many as 30,000 Igbos practicing some form of Judaism.

Akwa Ibom and Cross River Jews

The Annang, Efik and Ibibio people of Akwa Ibom and Cross River States of Nigeria have had ancient religious practices that strongly resembled some of the Jewish Torah. These include their traditional sacrifice of animals (rituals) by the presiding male of each village, or of a group of villages, for purification, especially during times of sickness.

European missionaries arriving in their land in the early 15th century called their religious practices "traditional religion".

However, they identify their religious practices and heritage with the Jews. They are believed to be members of the Northern Kingdom of Israel who left before the Babylonian captivity and migrated to the Efik/Ibibio/Annang land of Nigeria from Egypt via Ethiopia and Sudan. They have active synagogues with majority of the synagogues in the eastern part of the country a vibrant one in Abuja supported and provided with lots of Jewish materials by different Rabbis. There are also key Synagogues in Port Harcourt and Lagos. Synagogue services (Shabbat Services) of this region of Nigeria can be seen on the Internet, including the YouTube website.

Visiting Rabbis are always intrigued by some of the people's ability to read Hebrew fluently from Siddurim and Machzorim (Jewish Prayer books for Shabbat and high holidays) and also from Torah Scroll based on personal studies from various materials even without the presence of an internationally recognised Yeshivas (Jewish Institutions of study).

SIMILAR EGYPT   AND YORUBA WORDS TODAY AS A PROOF THAT YORUBA PEOPLE CAME FROM EGYPT
1. Wu (rise) Wu (rise)
2 Ere (python/ Serpent) Ere (Python / Serpent)
3. Horise (a great god) Orise (a great god)
4.Rekha (knowledge} Larikha (knowledge)
5.Unas (lake of fire) Una (fire)
6. Tan (complete) Tan (complete)
7.Beru (force of emotion) Beru (fear)
8.Bi (to become) Bi (to give birth, to become)
9 Kot (build) Ko (build)

Dr. Emmanuel Oluwole Adetula

10 Kot (boat) Oko (boat)

11. Omi (water) Omi (water)

12.Oni (title of Osiris) Oni (title of the king of Ife)

13. Budo (dwelling place) Budo (dwelling place)

14 Dudu (black image of Osiris) Dudu (black person)

15 Ra (possess) Ra (possess/buy)

16 Beka (pray/confess) Be or ka (to pray or confess)

17 Po (many) Po (many/cheap)

Moreover, with Israel coming under Greek, Persian and later Roman rule and dependency, renewed waves of Jewish refugees including traders and artisans began to set up more communities in Egypt, Cyrenaica, Nubia and the Punic Empire, notably in Carthage. From Carthage they began to scatter into various historically established, as well as newly emerging Jewish communities south of the Atlas mountains nearer to the modern day Mauritania, Niger, Mali, Nigeria, Senegal, Cameroon and Congo. Several Jewish nomadic groups also moved across the Sahara from Nubia and the ancient kingdom of Kush towards west Africa.

Various East and West African ethinic nations lay verifiable claim to their Jewish ancestral heritage. The Falashas, the most famous of those Black Jews have been validated. Close to three hundred thousand of those black Falasha Jews live in the modern State of Isreal as practising Jews.

The Lembas of South Africa, another so-called Bantu tribe have a cogent and valid claim to Jewish ancestory and heritage backed by solid genetic evidence i.e. the prevalence of the so-called Cohen modal J haplogroup. The Lembas as a group are indistinguishable from their Bantu neighbour's suggestiing that most Bantus groups possess this archetypal Jewish genetic haplogroup. It implies that there are potentially more bloodline Jews on the continent of Africa than anywhere else including modern Europe and Israel.

The names of old Jewish communities south of the Atlas mountains (around the regions of modern Niger, Nigeria), many of which existed well into Renaissance times, can be found in documents in synagogue archives in Cairo. See "George E. Lichtblau"

Jewish and Islamic chronicles cite the existence of Jewish rulers of certain Jewish tribal groups and clans (self identifying as Jewish) scattered throughout Mauritania, Senegal, the Western Sudan, Nigeria, and Ghana. See Ismael Diadie Haidara, "Les Juifs a'Timbouctou", Recueil de sources relatives au commerce juif a Timbouctou au XIXe siecle, Editions Donniya, Bamako, 1999.

According to the Tarikh es Soudan recorded by Abderrahman ben Abdallah es-Sadi (translated by O.Houdas) a Jewish community was formed by a group of Egyptian Jews, who had travelled to the West Africa through Chad. See also: al-Kati M., "Tarikh al-Fattash, 1600 ".

Another such community was located near the Niger River by the name of Koukiya led by a ruler known as Dia or Dji, a shortened form of "Dia min al Yaman" or Diallaiman (meaning he who comes from Yemen). According to local traditions, Diallaiman was a member of one of the Ethiopian-Jewish colonies transplanted from Yemen to Ethiopian-Abbysinia in the 6th century C.E. Dialliaman is said to have moved to West Africa along with his brother. They set up the Jewish community in Northern Nigeria

Dr. Emmanuel Oluwole Adetula

which later merged with the famous 7 Hausa States. See Meek C.K., "Northern Nigeria Tribes" Volume 1, Oxford, p.66.

A 9th century Jewish traveller Eldad ben-Mahli (also known as Eldad the Danite) related accounts about the location of some of the lost tribes of the House of Israel. According to this account, the tribe of Dan had migrated from Palestine so as not to take part in the internecine civil wars at the time of Yeroboam's succession. It was reported that this section was residing in the land of Havila beyond the waters of Ethiopia where there was much gold i.e. West Africa.

It was further reported that three other tribes had joined the tribe of Dan namely Naphtali, Gad, Asher. Those joined up with Dan in the land of Havila in the times of Sennacherib. They had an entire body of scriptures barring Esther and Lamentations. They neither used the Talmud nor the Mishna, but they had a Talmud of their own in which all the laws were cited in the name of Joshua the son of Nun. See Nahum Slouschz, "Travels in North Africa" Philadelphia 1927, p.227.

Ibn Khaldun, who lived in the 13th century, a respected authority on Berber history testified about the Black Jews of Western Sudan with whom he personally interacted. The famous muslim geographer al-Idrisi, born in Ceuta, Spain in the 12th century, wrote extensively about Jewish Negroes in the Western Sudan.

Black Jews were fully integrated and achieved pre-eminence in many West African kingdoms. For instance Jews were believed to have settled in great West African empires such as Songhai, Mali, Ghana and Kanem-Bornu empires. According to numerous accounts of contemporary visitors to the region several rulers, and administrators of the Songhai empire were of Jewish origins until Askia Muhammad came to power in 1492 and decreed that all Jews either convert to Islam or leave the region. See Ismael Diadie Haidara, "Les Juifs a'Timbouctou", Recueil de sources relatives au commerce juif a Timbouctou au XIXe siecle, Editions Donniya, Bamako, 1999.

The 16th century historian and traveler Leon Africanus, was a Hebrew-speaking Jewish convert to Islam, raised in a Jewish household by Jewish parents of Moroccan descent. Leon Africanus travelled extensively in Africa south of the Sahara where he encountered innumerable Black African Jewish communities. Leon later converted to Catholicism but remained interested in Jewish communities he encountered throughout his travels in West Africa. See Leo Africanus (al-Hassan b. al -Wazzan al-Zayyati), Della discrittione dell'Africa per Giovanni Leoni Africano, Settima Parte, in G.B. Ramusio, Delle navigationi e viaggi. Venice 1550, I, ff.78-81r.

Additional evidence is provided by surviving oral traditions of numerous African ethnic groups, including links to biblical ancestors, names of localities, and ceremonies with affinities to Jewish ritual practices. Moreover, the writings of several modern West African historians indicate that the memories of Jewish roots historical in West Africa continue to survive.

For instance, there are a number of historical records of small Jewish kingdoms and tribal groups known as Beni Israel that were part of the Wolof and Mandinge communities. These existed in Senegal from the early Middle Ages up to the 18th century, when they were forced to convert to Islam. Some of these claimed to be descendants of the tribe of Dan, the traditional tribe of Jewish gold and metal artisans, who are also said to have built the "Golden Calf".

Dr. Emmanuel Oluwole Adetula

Black Jews are said to have formed the roots of a powerful craft tradition among the still-renowned Senegalese goldsmiths, jewelers and other metal artisans. The name of an old Senegalese province called "Juddala" is said to attest to the notable impact Jews made in this part of the world. In addition to the Jewish tribal groups in Senegal who claim to be descendants of the tribe of Dan, the Ethiopian Jews also trace their ancestry to the tribe of Dan.

Additionally, Mr. Bubu Hama, a former president of the National Assembly in Niger and a prolific writer on African history has argued in many treatise as well as lecture tours that the Tuaregs had a Jewish queen in early medieval times, and that some Jewish Tuareg clans had preserved their adherence to that faith, in defiance of both Islamic and Christian missionary pressure, until the 18th century. In several of his books Hama cites the genealogies of Jewish rulers of the Tuareg and Hausa kingdoms. See "Lichtblau".

Some accounts place some West African Jewish community in the Ondo forest of Nigeria, south of Timbouctou. This community maintained a Torah Scroll as late as 1930s, written in Aramaic that had been burnt into parchment with a hot iron instead of ink so it could not be changed. See Gonen Rivaka, "The Quest for the Ten Lost tribes of Israel.

The Igbo's of Nigeria, one of the bigger nations that comprise Nigeria lay a strong claim to Jewish ancestry as borne out by their mores, laws, rituals and idioms which have a heavily accented old testament Hebrew flavor.

Ten Tribes of Israel that are Jewish in our World today!

Reuben, was not Jewish, but Hebrew (Israelites).
Simeon, was not Jewish, but Hebrew (Israelites).
Levi, was not Jewish, but Hebrew (Israelites).
Judah, Jewish, and also Hebrew, from who came the Jewish people,
from whom Yahshua (Jesus) was descended, who also was Jewish.
Zebulun, was not Jewish, but Hebrew (Israelites).
Dan, was not Jewish, but Hebrew (Israelites).
Gad, was not Jewish, but Hebrew (Israelites).
Asher, was not Jewish, but Hebrew (Israelites).
Naphtali, was not Jewish, but Hebrew (Israelites).
Joseph, Israelite, but Hebrew (Israelites).
Benjamin, was not Jewish, but Hebrew (Israelites).
Moses, Israelite, not Jewish, but Hebrew Exodus 2, 1-10. A descendent of Levi leads all 12 Tribes out of Egypt. Exodus 13:3.
Joshua, (Hoshea = Hebrew for 'Joshua' Numbers 13:8) descendent of Joseph, (called **'Ephraim'**) leads all 12 Tribes into the Promised Land, the land of Canaan. When the 12 Tribes of Israel entered the land, they were ruled by Judges and Kings. Then, because of Solomon's idolatries, Yahweh separated the tribes. He took away 10 Tribes (1 Kings chapters 11 and 12) calling them the Northern Kingdom, or Israel (also known as: Ephraim, Joseph or Jacob) while the two tribes, Benjamin and Judah are left in the land, and are called the Southern Kingdom, which became the Jewish people = descendents of Judah (house of David). (2 Kings 17:18 "...none left but the Tribe of Judahonly...)

After this division, the name 'Israel' from then on in the Old Testament refers only to the Northern Kingdom. Israel (known now as Ephraim, Joseph, or Jacob) are taken out of the land by

Dr. Emmanuel Oluwole Adetula

force, by the Assyrians 7035 B.C. 10% are left in the land of Samaria. Isaiah 6:12-13. The rest is history, they lost their identity, they became as Gentiles, a reason Jesus Christ raised up Paul the Apostle to preach to all the lost sheep of the house of Israel the Gentiles, so that in the last days all of us the Israelites who are now scattered in all parts of this planet in different nations with new identities will be gathered together in a new Kingdom of one world government on earth under the lordship and ruler ship of Jesus Christ the kings of Kings and Lord of Lords who is coming back again to this world for his own people.

The book of Revelation Chapter 21 says; And I saw a new heaven and a new earth; for the first heaven and the first earth were passed away; and there was no more sea, And the holy City **NEW JERUSALEM** (not this one in the middle east stained with the blood of Palestinians and Jewish women and children?) the bible says **a new Jerusalem,** prepared like a mobile home –ready like a bride, the tabernacle of God with men and Jesus will dwell again with men, we shall be his people and He will be our God, He will wipe away tears from our eyes, and in that day which is coming very soon, there shall be no more death, neither sorrow, nor crying, no more pain because all these politicians and their ways of doing things in ruling this world shall passed away. But the fearful, the murderers, the sorcerers and idolaters, and all liars will not be there, they shall go to hell where they belong. Will you be there? Where will you be my Brothers and Sisters, Ladies and Gentlemen when Jesus shall come? Think about it you all the lost tribes of Israel and let us get ready to come back home to the new Jerusalem where we shall all see his face.

Dome of the Rock, Jerusalem

THE DOME OF THE ROCK IN JERUSALEM

The city of Jerusalem is known in Arabic as *Al-Quds* or *Baitul-Maqdis* ("The Noble, Sacred Place"). Jerusalem is perhaps the only city in the world that is considered historically and spiritually significant to Jews, Christians, and Muslims alike. Perhaps you are wondering why Jerusalem is considered a holy city in Islam. Why is this place so important to Muslims? The Dome of the Rock is a Muslim shrine which stands on raised bedrock which is traditionally believed to be the place where the first Jewish temple was built. In the foreground of this photo we can see the el-Kas fountain which is connected to one of the largest of 49 cisterns underneath the Temple Mount area. Muslims come here to wash themselves prior to prayers within the mosque.

Jerusalem is known as the land of many prophets, peace be upon them all. Muslims revere all of the "Biblical" prophets, such as Abraham, Moses, David, Solomon, and Jesus - peace be upon them all. They all taught the Oneness of God.

Dr. Emmanuel Oluwole Adetula

First Qiblah for Muslims

Jerusalem was the first *Qiblah* for Muslims - the place toward which Muslims turn in prayer. It was many years into the Islamic mission (16 months after the Hijrah), that Muhammad (peace be upon him) was instructed to change the Qibla from Jerusalem to Mecca (Qur'an 2:142-144). It is reported that the Prophet Muhammad said, "There are only three mosques to which you should embark on a journey: the sacred mosque (Mecca, Saudi Arabia), this mosque of mine (Madinah, Saudi Arabia), and the mosque of Al-Aqsa (Jerusalem)."

Site of Night Journey and Ascension

It is Jerusalem that Muhammad (peace be upon him) visited during his night journey and ascension (called *Isra' and Mi'raj*). In one evening, the angel Gabriel miraculously took the Prophet from the Sacred Mosque in Mecca to the Furthest Mosque (Al-Aqsa) in Jerusalem. He was then taken up to the heavens to be shown the signs of God. The Prophet met with previous prophets and led them in prayer. He was then taken back to Mecca. The whole experience (which Muslim commentators take literally and Muslims believe as a miracle) lasted a few hours of a night. The event of Isra' and Mi'raj is mentioned in the Qur'an, in the first verse of Chapter 17 entitled 'The Children of Israel.'

"Glory to Allah, Who did take His servant for a journey by night, from the Sacred Mosque to the Farthest Mosque, whose precincts We did bless - in order that We might show him some of Our signs. For He is the One who hears and knows all things." (Qur'an 17:1)

This night journey further reinforced the link between Mecca and Jerusalem as holy cities, and serves as an example of every Muslim's deep devotion and spiritual connection with Jerusalem.

It is the hope of every Muslim that the Holy Land will be restored to a land of peace.

It was also here that people believe Abraham tried to sacrifice his son to God and where Muhammad is believed to have ascended into heaven in order to receive God's commandments. Constructed around 691 CE by Umayyad Dynasty, the Dome of the Rock has become the third holiest site for Muslim pilgrimage, after Mecca and Medina. It is probably the oldest surviving example of early Islamic architecture and is modeled after the Christian Church of the Holy Sepulcher, which is located nearby.

The compound has been central to nearly a century of conflict between Jews and Muslims in the region as both sides have battled over access rights, ownership, historical meaning and even spiritual value. The first major Jewish-Arab riots, in 1929, were sparked by conflict over access rights to Haram el Sharif. Muslims since 1948 have feared that Israeli Jews intend to destroy Al Aqsa in order to build another temple there.

When Jordan took control of Old Jerusalem in 1948, it barred Jews' access to the Temple Mount. After Israel occupied the Old City in 1967, it restored access and did not prevent Muslims from worshiping there. Conspiracy theories, however, abound

The mosque was set on fire by Michael Dennis Rohan, an Australian fundamentalist Christian, on Aug. 21, 1969. The mosque remains at the heart of Palestinian-Israeli tensions.

Dr. Emmanuel Oluwole Adetula

PRAYER FOR WORLD PEACE

Great God, who has told us
"Vengeance is mine,"
save us from ourselves,
save us from the vengeance in our hearts
and the acid in our souls.

Save us from our desire to hurt as we have been hurt,
to punish as we have been punished,
to terrorize as we have been terrorized.

Give us the strength it takes
to listen rather than to judge,
to trust rather than to fear,
to try again and again
to make peace even when peace eludes us.

We ask, O God, for the grace
to be our best selves.
We ask for the vision
to be builders of the human community
rather than its destroyers.
We ask for the humility as a people
to understand the fears and hopes of other peoples.

We ask for the love it takes
to bequeath to the children of the world to come
more than the failures of our own making.
We ask for the heart it takes
to care for all the peoples
of Afghanistan and Iraq, of Palestine and Israel
as well as for ourselves.

Give us the depth of soul, O God,

to constrain our might,
to resist the temptations of power
to refuse to attack the attackable,
to understand
that vengeance begets violence,
and to bring peace—not war—wherever we go.

For You, O God, have been merciful to us.
For You, O God, have been patient with us.
For You, O God, have been gracious to us.

And so may we be merciful
and patient
and gracious
and trusting
with these others whom you also love.

This we ask through Jesus,
the one without vengeance in his heart.
This we ask forever and ever. Amen

Until we meet again , I say the Lord bless you and keep you; The
Lord make his face shine upon you and be gracious to you; The Lord
turn his face toward you and give you peace. And please remember
always the word of Jesus Christ ; Blessed are the peacemakers: for
they shall be called the children of God. Blessed are they which are
persecuted for righteousness' sake: for theirs is the kingdom of
heaven.

Dr. Emmanuel O. Adetula. Peacemaker/Child of God.

Rededication Prayer

Father, I come to you in the name of Jesus. Your Word says, "Whosoever shall call on the name of the Lord shall be saved" (Acts 2:21). I am calling on you. I pray and ask Jesus to come into my heart and be Lord over my life according to Romans 10:9–10: "If thou shall confess with thy mouth the Lord Jesus, and shall believe in thine heart that God has raised him from the dead, thou shall be saved. For with the heart man believeth unto righteousness; and with the mouth confession is made unto salvation." I do that now. I confess that Jesus is Lord, and I believe in my heart that God raised him from the dead. I am now reborn! I am a Christian—a child of Almighty God! I am saved! In Jesus's name, amen!

Father, in the name of Jesus, your Word says if we confess our sins, you are faithful and just to forgive our sins and cleanse us from all unrighteousness (1 John 1:9). I confess my sins, and I thank you for your forgiveness and for cleansing me. Father, I desire a closer walk with the Lord. Your Word says if I draw closer to the Lord, he will draw closer to me (James 4:8).

Father, I rededicate my spirit, my mind, my soul, and my body back to you; and I ask you for a fresh anointing upon my whole life. I thank you for the blood of Jesus, which continually cleanses me from all unrighteousness! Thank you, Lord God, for allowing me to rededicate my life back to you. In Jesus's name, amen!

PRAYER OF DELIVERANCE

Father in the name of Jesus Christ of Nazareth in whom I believe, I plead the precious incorruptible blood of Jesus over myself, over my family and everything that belongs to me. I ask now for giant warrior angels to be loosed from heaven to surround and protect me. As your war agent and weapons of war in this earth planet I break down, undammed, and blow up all walls of protection around all my enemies, In the name of Jesus Christ I break down all walls around all witches, warlords, warlocks, Satanist, and the like that are against me, and I break the power of all curses, hexes, vexes, magic, voodoo, all mind control, jinxes, portions, bewitchments, death, destruction, sickness, pain, torment, physic power, physic warfare, evil prayer chains, and every evil thing else being sent my way or my family member way, or being sent against my business and my ministries way, and I return it now and the demons back to the senders right now!, SEVENFOLD, and I BIND it to them by the BLOOD OF JESUS ! In the name of JESUS. Amen.

I am free! It's DONE!

Dr. Emmanuel Oluwole Adetula

ABOUT THE AUTHOR

Dr. Emmanuel Adetula is best known for telling the truth and is counted among the most dynamic religious and social commentators in the making of a new world order. A religious leader and social entrepreneur with a master of arts in divinity, a doctor of philosophy in social work, and a holder of postgraduate certificates in negotiation and conflict management and Philanthropy from USIP in Washington, DC, and La Sierra University-Riverside, California. Emmanuel Oluwole Adetula, with many books to his credit, was born in Nigeria, West Africa, moved to United States as a legal permanent resident in 1999. He was director of the CCN House Community Development Agency in Los Angeles from 2002 to 2010, Founded CCN Center for Religious Peace and New World Order in 2011 , an organization whose mission is to seek and pursue good world governments, religious peace, liberty, and social justice by using research, dialogue, conferences, workshops, books, documentary films, TV and radio programs, Internet and social media as well as print media to achieve its mission in world communities. The organization promotion of the rule of law, transitional justice, and democracy features interviews and dialogues with political and religious leaders; the result of these dialogues contributed immensely to messages, speech, and sermons in Books, DVD, and CD formats. www.christchannelnetwork.com

How to Donate or Order a Copy of Emmanuel Books

CCN Center for Religious Peace is a division of Christ Channel Network (CCN) Inc., a bona fide 501(c) (3) nonprofit organization in the United States founded in 2002 by Dr. Emmanuel Adetula. He is in tremendous demand as one of the most dynamic speakers of our time. He receives invitations to speak in churches, colleges, and business corporations around the world.

If you are the one that God is talking to in helping to support this mission, do so today with your financial contribution of any amount that demonstrates your support for the ministry of Dr. Emmanuel Adetula and the Center for Religious Peace and New World Order.

Mail your donation to PO box 111589, Los Angeles, CA 90011, USA,

or visit our website to place your order for either the book or DVD or CD based on the cost of each item as listed on our website:

www.christchannelnetwork.com

All Emmanuel Adetula books available online at www.amazon.com

Search for Emmanuel Adetula books at www.amazon.com

Dr. Emmanuel Oluwole Adetula

www.ingramcontent.com/pod-product-compliance
Lightning Source LLC
LaVergne TN
LVHW021046210425
809190LV00017B/366